Embracing Social Media for Personal Growth

Table of Contents

We don't have a choice on whether we do social
media, the question is how well we do it.

— Erik Qualman

Chapter 1. Introduction

Ready to take your personal growth journey to a new level? Welcome to our Special Report - "Embracing Social Media for Personal Growth"! In this vibrant and captivating exploration, we bring to you a fresh perspective on harnessing the power of social media, a tool right at our fingertips, for the advancement of your personal and professional life. It's neither technical nor tedious. Instead, it's an energizing rise of sun on the dawn of your new chapter. We present not only the theory, but a wealth of real-life examples, interviews, and practical strategies to guide you every step of the way. This is not just another report you read - it's the key to unlocking the potential lying dormant within you. Get ready to level up, refresh your mindset, and grow like never before. So, are you excited to develop enriching connections, learn new skills, and turn your dreams into reality? Say goodbye to the old you and let's begin this exciting journey! Grab your copy, today!

Chapter 2. Discovering the Power of Social Media

As the curtain rises on the stage, we find ourselves peering into the robust world of social media, where personal and professional lives coalesce, blend, and sometimes blur. It's not just a digital landscape, nor a mere tool, but a reflection of the global society, where each individual paves their path towards growth, learning, and sometimes, reinvention. Let's together traverse this landscape, as we discover the inherent and immense power of social media.

2.1. Cracking Open the Social Media Spectrum

Firstly, it's essential to demystify the term 'social media'. Referring to a complex web of digital platforms, social media is where users create, share, and interact with the dynamic stream of information, while forming and nurturing connections. From Facebook to LinkedIn, Instagram to TikTok, Twitter to Snapchat, each platform has a unique set of functionalities and intended audience, aligning with diverse needs, interests, and communication preferences.

2.2. How Social Media Influences Lives

Social media's influence transcends not only geographical boundaries but also personal ones. It rolls out the red carpet towards a stroll in the global digital village. From learning cooking recipes on YouTube to partaking in intellectual conversations on Twitter, foraying into a beautiful world of images on Instagram to forging professional connections on LinkedIn — the possibilities are endless. The real potential of social media lies in its ability to project our voice, reflect our identity, and shape our perception while fostering learning, change, and growth.

2.3. The Social Media Landscape

The social media landscape is more than just a digital smorgasbord of platforms. It is as diverse as the human conversation itself. With big-tent platforms like Facebook and Instagram, which infuse users' daily lives with entertainment, camaraderie, and information exchange, to more specific platforms like LinkedIn and Medium, facilitating career-related discussions and content creation, the landscape keeps evolving. Platforms like Snapchat and TikTok redefine the way younger generations communicate and consume content, while Pinterest and Instagram have carved their niche in the domains of lifestyle, fashion, and DIY endeavours.

2.4. Empowering Tools Of Personal Expression

In essence, social media profiles are dynamic, digital portfolios capturing the persona behind the screen. The platforms become arenas for personal expression, showcasing interests, sentiments, ideologies, and showcasing 'human-ness.' They grant individuals the power to control the narrative around their identity, providing strategic tools for image-building and personal branding. From the quintessential LinkedIn profile to an aesthetically curated Instagram feed, the public persona we shape in cyberspace significantly affects how we are perceived in the digital society.

2.5. Impact on Personal Growth

Social media's impact on personal growth is vast. It facilitates self-exploration, provides avenues for learning, aids personal development, and cultivates networks fostering career advancement. The interactive models push the users to introspect, recognise their preferences, and identify their aspirations. They encourage establishing enriching connections and contribute positively to their personal and professional lives. The numerous resources available on such platforms, including tutorials, courses, lectures, and skill-sharing content, can directly fuel personal growth initiatives.

2.6. Powering Transformation

Finally, the transformative power of social media should not be underestimated. It empowers users to shape their destinies. It offers unimaginable potential to turn passive consumers into active creators, bystanders into influencers, and dreamers into achievers. It's quite empowering to know that you hold in your hands the switch to illuminate your path of personal growth.

As we embark on this voyage into the vibrant world of social media, we must pay heed to one poignant truth - social media, in all its might, remains a tool, the power of which lies in usage. The potential for personal growth is not woven into the infrastructure of the social media platforms but, instead, it's crafted meticulously by the users themselves who harness these platforms' power strategically and judiciously. This intricate intertwining of personal intention, strategic use, and the environment's empowerment brings forth the beautiful tapestry of personal growth thorugh social media, the subtext of the entire digital revolution we're living today.

Consider this your invitation, a gentle nudge towards acknowledging the power of social media and its potential in driving personal growth, fuelling aspirations, and fulfilling dreams. As you delve further into this exploration, remember that the power lies with you, the user, waiting to be discovered and wielded for your betterment. As we move forward, brace yourself to delve deeper into understanding the functionalities and strategies to harness the power that lies in your hands, a power that has the potential to transform you and lead to exponential personal growth.

Chapter 3. Building a Positive Digital Identity

In today's digital age, where a vast number of interactions and transactions happen over the internet, our digital identity has become an indispensable part of our lives. Your digital identity can be described as the online persona you craft for yourself and project to the world using social media channels. It reflects who you are or, at times, who you intend to portray yourself to be in the online realm. When strategically and conscientively curated, a positive digital identity can act as a catalyst in your personal and professional growth. Let's get started and unravel how this can be done.

3.1. Understanding the Essence of a Digital Identity

In essence, your digital identity embodies all information available online about you. This ranges from basic details such as your name, age, and occupation, to more detailed elements like your interests, affiliations, and public sentiments. This also incorporates any data linked to online actions, such as clicks, likes, posts, shares, comments, and even passive browsing activities.

All these fragments of information collectively form your online identity, providing an image of who you are in the virtual arena. Effectively managing this digital persona paves the way to mastering digital citizenship, which refers to responsible, respectful, and ethical behavior in the digital world.

3.2. Crafting a Positive Online Persona

How you present yourself online massively influences how others perceive you. Painting a positive image of yourself on social media requires substantial discretion and consistency over time. Start by reflecting on your values, passions, and aspirations. Allow these aspects to reflect in the content you share, the comments you make, and the interactions you engage in on these platforms.

It's crucial to remain authentic while catering your online image, as authenticity often leads to relatability and genuine connections. As you continue, ensure you're not overposting or oversharing, as this may dilute your message or compromise your privacy.

Online etiquette, or 'netiquette', is yet another cornerstone of a positive digital image. Express your opinions respectfully, practice empathetic commenting, and avoid participating in online bullying or hate speech.

3.3. One's Career and Online Persona

Your social media presence has considerable implications on your professional journey too. Prospective employers often perform online background checks on candidates; a strong and positive online identity could thus be a distinct advantage. Showcase your skills, achievements, and experiences through platforms like LinkedIn to enhance your employability.

Participation in online communities related to your field of work can also underline your dedication and proactive attitude. For instance, joining forums for writers or developers exposes you to a rich resource of learning and networking opportunities.

3.4. Enforcing Online Privacy

While building a positive online identity, it's absolutely critical to exercise particular diligence towards safeguarding your privacy. Regularly review and update your privacy settings across different platforms. Be cautious while sharing sensitive information online. Strong password practices coupled with a good understanding of your digital footprint can greatly assist in keeping your identity safe.

3.5. Embracing the Art of Digital Forgiveness

With digital identities etching a near-permanent mark in cyberspace, it's essential to remember that we all evolve. Something you posted years ago might not reflect who you are today. The concept of digital forgiveness encourages understanding this evolution and accepting that past errors don't necessarily define present identities.

In conclusion, curating a positive digital identity is a continuous process. It entails self-awareness, thoughtful communication, and constant learning. As you navigate the digital landscape, always remember - your digital identity reflects who you are. Make it positive, make it count.

Chapter 4. Using Social Media for Self-Discovery

The evolution of social media platforms has ushered in an era where everyone has a global stage at their fingertips. The opportunity to send your voice to every corner of the world is no longer restricted to moguls or reserved to media giants. However, beyond the noise, the likes, the shares, and the trending hashtags, lies a much subtler and tremendously powerful facet of social media - the conduit of personal self-discovery. Through this channel, we shape and discover our values, interests, aspirations, and effectively, our identities in this virtual space.

4.1. Crafting A Social Media Mirror

A mirror reveals our physical form, but the screen of our social media reflects something deeper — our thoughts, beliefs, interests, and values. And as any mirror, it could either be a truthful reflection of who we are or a distorted image shaped by societal norms, expectations, or our desire for validation.

There's immense power in using social media as a mirror of introspection, reflecting our authentic selves. It requires honesty to admit our likes and dislikes, courage to share our views, and humility to accept feedback. Engage with content that prompts you to think, reflect, and respond, not just consume passively. Look back at your past posts, interactions, comments. Do they align with your core values? They can offer valuable insights into your evolving self and even rake up forgotten passions and interests.

4.2. Building Your Virtual Community

Having the right people in your network can significantly shape your self-discovery process. Surrounding yourself with diverse thinkers, passionate individuals, thought leaders can inspire new ideas, broaden your horizon, and challenge your perspective in positive ways. Carefully curated exposure to diverse topics and discussions promotes introspection, fostering your growth. However, discernment is key. The illusion of social media can persuade us to project a life that is trending rather than one that's authentically ours. Embrace connections that resonate with your authentic self, ones that fuel your growth and stimulate inspiring conversations.

4.3. Embracing Constructive Feedback

Social media allows us to put our thoughts, creations, and perspectives out for the world to see, inevitably opening ourselves to criticism and, crucially, constructive feedback. This feedback can be invaluable in our journey of self-discovery. However, it's also crucial to differentiate constructive criticism from destructive negativity. Remember, don't let someone's comment on your post define you or your worth. Feedback is just another perspective, not an absolute truth.

4.4. Expressing Yourself Authentically

In crafting our posts, pictures, stories, and videos, we get to explore who we are and what matters to us. It's a chance to discover and present our unique voice, perspective, and style. That being said, portraying a consistent image should never come at the cost of authenticity. While it can be invigorating to showcase a well-curated life, remember, it's perfectly fine to share your struggles, doubts, and raw moments. It's these unfiltered pieces of ourselves that build genuine connections and encourage authentic self-expression.

4.5. Exploring New Frontiers

In the vast virtual landscape, there are always new avenues to explore. New platforms, groups, or initiatives can spark interests you weren't even aware of, leading to surprising discoveries about yourself. Explore and engage with a wide array of content. Follow different people, join diverse groups, start conversations on topics that intrigue you.

Social media is much more than just a platform for virtual connectivity; it's a dynamic, rich ground for self-discovery. By looking beyond the surface, practicing conscious engagement, we can harness social media's power to understand ourselves better. It allows us to examine our beliefs, understand our values, and uncover hidden layers of our personality. But remember, while social media serves as a tool for self-discovery, it should not dictate your self-worth or identity. You're much more than a profile on a screen, likes on a post, or followers on your feed. Your journey of self-discovery on social media is about you, and the person you uncover should be the one you're most comfortable with - your authentic self.

Chapter 5. The Art of Connecting: Network and Relationships

As we step into the sphere of social media, it's impossible not to take notice of the significance of connections, networks, and relationships that are built, nurtured, and advanced within these digital spaces. These integral components of social media, when well understood and strategically utilized, can spur personal growth in an astonishingly transformative way. As you take this journey of understanding the art and science behind creating profound connections and fostering meaningful relationships on social media, keep in mind the cardinal tenet - It's not about how many connections you make, but about how many people you connect with.

5.1. Decoding Connection: Starting at Square One

Connections on social media comprise people you associate with, learn from, interact with, and possibly even grow with. These connections could range from high school friends, colleagues, mentors, inspirational figures, to potential employers or partners. The number of connections you have might reflect your influence on social media, but it's the quality of these connections and the profoundness of your relationships with them that truly transforms your personal growth journey.

To begin connecting, start by engaging. You can engage by liking, commenting, and sharing posts. Be authentic in your engagements. Authenticity in interactions not only strengthens connections but also fosters trust and respect. You could also explore mutually beneficial relationships by supporting and amplifying others' messages while hoping for reciprocation. Remember, it's all about give and take!

Another approach to filter potential connections is through common interest groups. These groups host discussions on focused topics where you can share your ideas, engage in enriching debates, and learn from different perspectives.

5.2. Building a Network: The Power of Community

Building a social media network isn't just about amassing followers or connections, it's about creating a sense of community among individuals who share common interests, goals, or beliefs. Practically, people perceive social media networks as platforms for broadcasting their lives. However, viewing it as a community-building tool opens up opportunities for deeper engagement, learning, and growth.

Start by following influencers or thought leaders in your area of interest. Engage with their content, but more importantly, interact with their audience. Discussions under their posts could be gold mines for expanding your network with like-minded individuals.

While building your network, be open to diverse thoughts. Include people from various fields, cultures, and backgrounds. Diverse networks promote intellectual growth, challenge your thinking, and often lead to innovative ideas.

5.3. Cultivating Relationships: Beyond Connections

A relationship goes beyond a casual interaction or connection—it's the establishment of shared values, experiences, and goals.

Relationships on social media are the meaningful interactions that occur over time between you and your connections.

To cultivate relationships, a great starting point is sharing valuable content that resonates with your network. Regularly posting thought-provoking content sparks conversations, encourages dialogue, and deepens relationships built on valuable exchanges of ideas.

Remember that social media is an extension of real life. Responding to comments, showing empathy, celebrating others' triumphs, and offering help in challenging times all demonstrate care and nurture relationships.

Fostering relationships also involves maintaining balance. While it's essential to express your views, it's equally important to be an active listener. Being open to learning and respecting differing on views fuels conversations and solidifies relationships,—a concept that should be embraced in both the virtual and real world.

5.4. Nurturing Professional Relationships: Career Growth through Networking

Social media can be a powerful advancement tool in your career by nurturing professional relationships. Platforms like LinkedIn allow you to connect with industry professionals, employers, and thought leaders, which can present you with opportunities for mentorship, collaborations, and even job opportunities.

Actively partaking in professional discussions, sharing industry-related content, and showcasing your skills and achievements can attract the attention of potential employers or partners. Regular meetups, webinars, and virtual workshops are also powerful mediums to network professionally.

These are but the prime steps towards mastering the art of connecting. As you traverse this path, you're bound to discover novel strategies and approaches which resonate with you and your personal growth journey. In the grand scheme of things, social media might be just a platform, but it's not about the platform; it's all about the people. The relationships you build and treasure on these platforms might start as digital connections, but they have the potential to forge into lifelong relationships. Channelizing the power of social media to connect, network, and cultivate relationships inherently unlocks a world of limitless learning, growth, and opportunities.

Chapter 6. Social Media as a Learning Tool

In the modern age, where technology is threaded with virtually every aspect of our daily experiences, social media has emerged as a powerful learning tool. Not only is it perpetually accessible, but it offers an infinite library of resources, insights, and inspiration. From helping us acquire new skills and understanding complex concepts to keeping us updated on global trends, consider how social media helps shape and spur the ceaseless pursuit of knowledge.

6.1. Utilizing Social Media to Acquire New Skills

Social media cauldron brims with a vast array of online courses, video tutorials, webinars, and instructional posts, making it a potential goldmine for skill acquisition. Platforms like LinkedIn offer myriad learning paths specifically designed for skill betterment in several areas from digital marketing to data science. Acclaimed experts share insightful online tutorials on Youtube, helping millions grasp complex concepts with ease. Instagram isn't far behind, with its captivating infographic posts that simplify labyrinthine theories into digestible chunks of information. Hence, social media has revolutionized self-paced education, bringing the classroom to your pocket.

6.2. Expanding Your Knowledge Base through Expert Insights

On social media platforms, global scholars, thought-leaders, and industry experts willingly share their perspectives, research findings, and game-changing innovations. They often participate in live sessions, tweet insightful threads, share thought-provoking blogs, or publish LinkedIn articles. By following these knowledgeable personas, we have an opportunity to learn directly from the industry's best minds, expanding our understanding and molding informed perspectives.

6.3. Staying Up-to-date with Latest Trends and Global Conversations

Social media platforms like Twitter have become renowned sources for real-time updates on international happenings, technological breakthroughs, and trending conversations. With its unique hashtag feature, finding and following discussions concerning your interests have never been easier. Such active participation nurtures critical thinking and helps us stay abreast of the rapidly evolving world.

6.4. Harnessing the Power of Peer Learning

The art of learning is a nuanced tapestry woven with many threads, with peer learning being a prominent strand. Platforms like Facebook Groups or Reddit Subreddits serve as online forums where ideas, insights, and experiences are exchanged freely, creating a peer learning environment. Here, we can post queries, engage in discussions, share resources, and learn from the collective wisdom of the community.

6.5. From Passive Scrolling to Active Learning

Just as we value mindful living, the concept of mindful browsing brings about a paradigm shift in our social media habits. Instead of aimlessly scrolling through feeds, redirecting our focus to academic resources, skill-building content, knowledge-enriching profiles and pages can transform social media into a virtual learning hub.

6.6. Overcoming the Noise: Finding Authentic and Reliable Information

In this sea of information, distinguishing between authentic and inaccurate information becomes crucial. Follow verified accounts, maintain a diversified following list, read from multiple sources, and cross-verify facts to ensure the credibility of the information you consume.

In conclusion, if used effectively, social media can be an incredibly potent learning tool, forever altering the dynamics of our knowledge acquisition. Remember, the aim is not about the amount of information consumed, but the valuable insights and skills we derive from it. Tailoring our experience to suit our learning needs can help us unlock the enormous potential that social media has to offer for personal growth and lifelong learning.

Chapter 7. Harnessing Social Media for Career Advancement

Social media platforms have experienced an unprecedented surge in popularity over the past decade, geared by progress in internet access and smartphone technology. They've evolved from simple tools connecting friends and family to vast communities engaging billions of active users worldwide. Nowadays, social media platforms offer a unique opportunity to play an integral role in career advancement. The following expose dives into the intricate dimensions of constituting and fine-tuning your social media presence for the same.

7.1. Social Media Platforms: The Modern Job Market

The first point to appreciate about harnessing social media for your career prospects is that it's rapidly transforming into a pivotal component of the modern job market. These platforms provide unprecedented access to fellow professionals, industry leaders, potential employers, and job opportunities that previously might never have popped up on your radar. LinkedIn, Twitter, Facebook, and even Instagram now feature job postings alongside their primary offerings with more frequency than ever before. To summarize, social media has fully-imprinted itself on the structure of the contemporary job market.

However, browsing through job postings is only a fraction of how one can tap into social media's potential. In the current era, where personal branding holds astonishing importance, our digitized personas shouldn't just be given a once-over before a job interview.

Prospective employers and professional connections are more than likely glimpsing through your profiles at some point or other. So, it's paramount to portray an appeal that extends beyond a traditional resume.

7.2. Building and Maintaining a Positive Online Persona

Building a positive online portfolio is crucial for creating opportunities for career advancement. This fundamental shift shies away from the confines of a 2-page curriculum vitae (CV) and promotes a more organic, comprehensive image of their potential employee. It involves maintaining a meticulous, yet authentic digital blueprint of your professional life, including experiences, values, and aspirations.

Sharing articles, publications, trends, and observations relevant to your industry portrays you as a current, involved, and informed professional. Engaging in online debates, starting fruitful discussions, and demonstrating leadership or subject matter expertise through original content are other ways to enrich your online persona. All these activities, wrapped in professional decorum and respectful communication, can make an indelible impression.

Always remember, your online canvas should not only be filled with your professional journey but also with hues of your personality, philosophical perspectives, and societal values. A balanced blend of professional accomplishments and personal interests serves as a comprehensive portrayal to possible employers.

7.3. Networking: Building Bridges to Opportunities

Networking is another distinctive advantage of social media platforms. They provide access to an unbounded network of professionals across the globe, where strategic connections are the bridges leading you to your dream job. Networking through social media platforms ensures a continuous flow of opportunities even when you aren't actively job hunting.

Remember, networking is a two-way street. Don't always wait for others to initiate conversations—be proactive. Engage with others' posts, offer meaningful comments, and participate in group discussions. However, remember, the ultimate goal is not simply to gain a high number of connections but to establish robust professional relationships marked by mutual enrichment.

7.4. Balancing Personal and Professional Life on Social Media

While sharing personal information might help paint a more dimensional and human image, it is essential to avoid crossing over into the realm of oversharing. In this digital era, where lines between personal and professional lives are increasingly blurred, maintaining a certain degree of separation is a safe and respectful approach. After all, a professional network might not be the best place to share every aspect of your personal life.

Maintain a tactful balance in what you share. Focus on authenticity and allow your personality to shine, but refrain from sharing anything that could be deemed inappropriate or harmful to your professional image. An easy check is to simply ask, before posting, how you'd feel if a potential employer viewed the shared content.

7.5. Learning and Growing: Nourish Your Knowledge via Social Media

Lastly, career advancement via social media is not just limited to job hunting or networking; it is also about ongoing learning. As platforms crowded with professionals from various walks of life share their expertise, thoughts, experiences, and knowledge, these platforms transform into a treasure trove of wisdom. Make it a habit to learn from the vast array of resources available to you.

Extracting career value from social media requires a strategic, thoughtful approach—understanding that it's more than just a place for leisurely browsing. Used efficiently, these platforms can cater to all fundamental aspects of career advancement: job search, networking, personal branding, and continuous learning. Hence, making social media a cornerstone in your career advancement strategy can yield unprecedented results.

Harnessing social media for career advancement is a continuous process rather than a one-time effort. Remember, consistency is key. Continuous refinement of your social media strategy, constantly learning, sharing your insights, and building meaningful professional relationships, are what will ultimately keep you on your chosen path of personal and professional growth.

Chapter 8. Avoiding Pitfalls: Social Media Missteps to Learn From

Despite the near-ubiquitous nature of social media and its undeniable potential for fostering personal growth and professional development, it is not a journey devoid of risks and challenges. There exist a myriad of pitfalls that can trip up even the most seasoned users; learning how to navigate these obstacles is vital towards optimizing your experience.

8.1. Understanding the Nature of Social Media

To begin our exploration, it's pertinent to delve into the core characteristics of social media, as these features breed both the advantages and potential downfalls this platform can provide. Social media, by nature, is a public medium intended for the sharing of information, ideas, personal messages, and other content such as images, audio, and video. It thrives on its ability to connect diverse individuals, regardless of geographic location. Yet, the very accessibility that gives social media its global reach can also familiarize you with dangers such as the potential divulgence of one's privacy and the risk of misinformation.

Navigation through social media calls for informed decisions at every step. A single post, shared hastily, can have ramifications lasting beyond what one might anticipate.

8.2. Privacy Concerns

In an attempt to gain followers, likes, and comments, social media users often overlook one critical aspect of their online persona - maintaining their privacy. Every piece of information you disclose, no matter how trivial it might seem, adds to the digital trail you leave behind. This information is accessible to every individual and can often lead to cyber stalking, identity theft or data mining.

To counter these risks, it's necessary to be selective about the information you share - both in your profile details, and in the content of your posts. Additionally, regularly update your privacy settings to keep abreast with social media platform's evolving policies.

8.3. The Spread of Misinformation

One of the most significant challenges for social media users is the dissemination of fake news and misinformation. This becomes especially detrimental when it affects your perception of the world or causes you to take ill-advised actions based on falsehoods.

Therefore, treat every piece of information with skepticism. Probe into the authenticity of the source, investigate the facts, and consider the impacts before spreading information further.

8.4. Cyberbullying and Online Harassment

Social media must be a safe space fostering positivity and personal growth. However, the anonymous nature of the internet makes it an accessible platform for bullies. It's crucial to recognize and proactively combat cyberbullying whenever you encounter it.

Steps towards this include blocking or reporting such users and maintaining an empathetic, respectful online demeanor.

8.5. Social Media Addiction

While social media can accelerate personal growth, overuse can lead to addiction, disconnection from real-life relationships and mental health issues. It is, therefore, necessary to strike a balance between digital and real-world experiences. Setting dedicated hours for social media, disconnecting regularly, and prioritizing offline interactions can help in mitigating these risks.

Now, with a keen understanding of social media's potential pitfalls, the road to personal development doesn't seem as perilous. Remember that social media is what you make of it. It can be an excellent tool for personal growth and communication if used judiciously, but can also engulf users within its negative aspects if left unchecked. By recognizing and avoiding these pitfalls, your engagement on social media can evolve from a minefield of risks to a garden of possibilities, enabling your personal growth to flourish.

Chapter 9. Navigating Social Media Challenges: Privacy, Security, and Balance

Maneuvering through the labyrinth of social media does present a variety of challenges that often revolve around three major areas: privacy, security and maintaining an appropriate balance between consumption and creation. The reality of the digital age mandates an understanding and careful navigation through these arenas. This section of the report will delve deeply into each area, delineating actionable strategies and indispensable tools to make your digital voyage both secure and enriching.

9.1. The Privacy Conundrum: Staying Invisible in the Digital Spotlight

In a world where oversharing has become the norm, maintaining privacy has become a complex task. It is important to be aware that when you share content on social media, you are essentially publishing information that can be accessible to anyone.

Here, context is king. Be certain to fine-tune the privacy settings on your social media accounts to limit who has viewing permissions. Make judicious use of settings that allow the blurring between public and private to be heavily tilted in your favour. A practical tip is to use 'Friends Only' or 'Followers Only' features wherever available, as they limit your audience to a certain group that you have already vetted.

Moreover, a significant aspect of privacy is also about managing personal information. Be careful not to divulge sensitive details like address, contact number, financial information etc., unless absolutely necessary and only on secure platforms. Learn to differentiate between necessary disclosure and avoidable exposure.

9.2. Unleashing the Security Shield: Protecting Data and Detering Dangers

Security threats lurk in every corner of the digital world. From scammers to hackers and viruses, the challenges are diverse, but a strong line of defense can be built.

Start by creating strong, unique passwords for your accounts. Consider using password managers that securely store your passwords and generate complex new ones. They are a great tool in maintaining security without stressing your memory.

Two-factor authentication (2FA) is another layer of security you ought to deploy. It's a simple way to confirm your identity by providing two pieces of evidence that you indeed are the rightful owner of the account. This often is a combination of something you know (like a password) and something you receive or have (like a code sent to your phone).

Regularly updating the software on your devices also aids security as updates often include patches for newly discovered security vulnerabilities. Lastly, be mindful of the links you click on, the apps you download, and the permissions you give.

9.3. Steadying the Seesaw: Striking the Right Balance between Consumption and Creation

Balance is critical in almost every aspect of our life. Social media is no exception. Finding the sweet spot between consumption and creation is paramount to productive and nourishing social media usage.

On the consumption side, it is important to curate your feeds mindfully. Tidy up your digital space just as you would keep your physical environment clutter-free. Unfollow pages or people that don't serve your growth or trigger negativity. Instead, choose to follow accounts that align with your aims, inspire you, enlighten you, or challenge you in healthy ways. Draw a line between informed and overwhelmed, between entertainment and waste of time.

On the creation side, consider quality over quantity. Sharing your thoughts, projects, or life's highlights can be fulfilling and helpful to others. However, do not get swept by the 'posting pressure.' It's not a competition. Treat it as a platform to express, learn, and connect, rather than impress.

Make mindful decisions about when and how often you engage with social media. Apps often have built-in features to limit your screen time or remind you to take breaks. Make use of these to ensure you do not get sucked into the vortex of endless scrolling.

In conclusion, as you employ these strategies, you are no longer battling with social media complexities but dancing with them. Your transformative journey to leverage social media for personal growth suddenly becomes safer, private, yet open and balanced in an empowering way. From here on, you will bear the torch of digital literacy, bringing light not only to your path but also illuminating the way for others.

Chapter 10. Transition from Consumption to Creation: Becoming a Social Media Maven

As the clock hand completes another cycle, and you find yourself nestled deeper into the fabric of social media navigation, it's time to explore the profound transition from consumer to creator. This idiosyncratic part of your journey amplifies your perseverance and creativity, enabling you to step forth as a lodestar that others look to for guidance, inspiration, and knowledge. This new contributor's role you're transitioning into - the social media maven as it's known - can seem daunting initially but remember, every expert was once a beginner.

10.1. The Journey from Consumption to Creation

To genuinely comprehend this transition, you should, first and foremost, understand the difference between consumers and creators. The former refers to those who predominantly absorb and interact with content created by others. Consumers often adopt a passive role, like a spectator or a bystander, within the social media ecosystem, primarily feasting on the information disseminated by creators.

On the contrary, creators embark on the more adventurous route, creating original content and engaging more proactively with their peers. They chart the terrain of social media by constantly generating novel content, which could span a trove of forms from blog posts, infographics, and case studies to podcasts, vlogs, and live-streams.

Furthermore, creators aspire to mold perceptions, incite change or simply offer a fresh viewpoint on a subject.

Your journey from being a consumer to a creator will require a bit of courage, a pinch of creativity, and a dab of determination. Also, the understanding that the voyage is seldom linear constitutes an integral part of this transition. There will be numerous trials and experiments, stumbles and learning as you hone your voice and discover your niche.

10.2. Crafting Your Creator Identity

Commit to your niche. It's vital to choose a subject you are fashioned out of love and expertise. This focused approach not only helps to develop a cohesive brand but also attracts the right kind of audience and fosters genuine connections. The niche should echo your passion and align with your personal as well as professional aspirations.

Maintaining a regular timetable for creation and sticking to it invariably multiplies your efficacy and audience engagement. Consistency lets your audience know what to expect, and over time, builds their trust in you. Be patient; understand it's not an overnight process. Cultivating an engaged audience, chiseling your creative prowess and building your virtual empire on authenticity takes time.

Rafting through the river of self-doubt is another vital aspect in crafting your creator's identity. It's common to feel apprehensive about putting your work out there. To counteract this, focus on creating value rather than seeking validation. Engage with empathy, celebrate your little victories, and keep in mind that your work is influencing at least one person positively.

10.3. Exploring Content Formats and Channels

Not all content formats are created equal, and neither are they universally suitable. Whether you lean more towards writing, speaking, or visual artistry can significantly affect your choice of format and platform.

If ideas flow more voluntarily into written words, blogging, guides, ebooks, or tweet threads might be your go-to formats. A passion for speaking could translate into successful podcasts or live streams, while a knack for visuals, design, or any form of visual storytelling might manifest as infographics, photography, or short films.

Similarly, different social media platforms uniquely cater to various types of content. For instance, Instagram and YouTube are ideal for visual or video format, LinkedIn for professional content, Twitter for short, pithy takes on reality, and Medium or WordPress for lengthy, thoughtful pieces. The key is to match your content format to the platform that best suits it.

10.4. Building an Engaged Audience

Building an audience is one of the most exciting aspects of becoming a social media maven. You are not only creating a following but a community of like-minded individuals who respect, learn, and grow from your shared knowledge.

Engagement is the lifeblood of this endeavor. Respond to comments, ask questions, create polls, encourage debates; anything that doesn't just spark dialogue, but also keeps it ignited. Building a sense of community around your brand and making your followers feel heard, recognized, and importantly, valued, are critical to maintain an engaged audience.

10.5. Lessons from Successful Creators

Learning from those who have traversed this path before you can provide invaluable insights. Some of the most successful social media creators emphasize the importance of being authentic, telling unique stories, focusing on value over validation, committing to a niche, consistency, and lastly, and perhaps most importantly, a willingness to persist even when things don't appear promising.

10.6. Keeping Up with Trends and Constant Evolution

The digital world is in a state of constant flux, with new user patterns, trending topics, algorithms, and platforms emerging at a dazzling speed. To keep your content fresh and engaging, staying abreast of these changes, and finding instinctive ways to incorporate them into your work is critical.

But remember, while trends could give your content a momentary boost, it's essential that your focus remains on crafting original work that reflects your true self. Molding your ideals and content to each passing trend can be counterproductive and veer you off-course.

10.7. Ensuring a Sustainable Journey

Ensure this journey is a marathon, not a sprint. Focus on evolving without burning out and maintain a healthy creator-audience relationship, which does not strain your mental or physical health. Ensure to strike a balance between your virtual and real life, creativity, and consumption; between engaging with your audience and taking time for your self-care and development.

Remember, the journey from consumption to creation isn't just about content creation or garnering followers. It's an inward journey of self-discovery, growth, and asserting your voice in the world, one post at a time. As you move ahead, embrace the iterations and remember, the world needs your unique narrative.

So, gear up, create, and share your light with the world as you transition into becoming a true social media maven.

Chapter 11. Keeping Momentum: Sustaining Personal Growth Through Social Media

In the captivating narrative of personal growth through social media, one final hurdle often eludes us - sustaining momentum. Because after the first taste of empowerment and success using these fantastic platforms, how do we continue the journey, keeping the fire of continuous learning and evolution alive? This chapter is an exhaustive exploration of that, from understanding the importance to equipping yourself with concrete strategies.

11.1. Importance of Sustained Growth

A fundamental philosophy in life underscores that whenever you stop growing, you start dying. True growth is consistent, that doesn't lose momentum, no matter the circumstances. It's a journey, not a destination. In the context of personal growth through social media, the philosophy isn't any different. Continuous learning, constant engagement, and frequent interaction should be the way of life on these platforms. But a fair share of challenges can obstruct that journey - losing interest, plateauing learning, or simply getting overwhelmed with information. Learning how to surmount these challenges can help in ensuring sustained growth.

11.2. Keeping the Fire of Curiosity Alive

At the heart of sustained personal growth lies an eternal flame – the fire of curiosity. Curiosity fuels the desire to learn, motivates the pursuit of knowledge, and drives engagement and interaction on social media platforms. But how does one keep this fire alive in a sea of constant digital information?

- Engage Regularly: Ignite your curiosity by staying active on various platforms. Join discussions, ask questions, share insights, and follow thought leaders.

- Explore New Niches: Venture out of your comfort zone. Dabble in unfamiliar topics and challenge your perspectives.

- Foster a Growth Mindset: Cultivate a mindset that embraces learning and growth. Remember, mistakes are lessons, not failures.

11.3. Leveraging Social Media for Continuous Learning

Social media can be a crown jewel for continuous learning if reported. Here are some strategies:

- Participating in Webinars and Live Discussions: Platforms like LinkedIn, Twitter and Facebook host numerous webinars, live discussions, and chats facilitated by industry experts. Participate actively.

- Online Courses and Certificates: Many educational institutions and organizations offer online classes and certificates across numerous disciplines through social media. Embrace these opportunities.

- Use Tools for Learning: Most platforms have features for educational purposes. For instance, LinkedIn Learning, Facebook's educational videos, or Instagram's insightful infographics.

11.4. Overcoming Plateauing

The journey of continuous learning can sometimes hit a roadblock, or a 'plateau.' Here, despite engaging, the knowledge curve doesn't grow. Here's how to address it:

- Break Routine: Alter your interaction patterns or learn a completely new skill. The novelty can break the learning stalemate.

- Co-learn and Co-create: Engage with the community in learning something new or creating something together.

- Seek Expert Help: Connect with subject matter experts or mentors who can guide you.

11.5. Avoiding Information Overload

In our quest to grow, we must beware of information overload. Consuming information indiscriminately can lead to exhaustion and reduce productivity. Implement strategies like curating content, managing time effectively on social media, and taking regular digital detoxes to maintain a healthy engagement.

11.6. Sustained growth and the Bigger Picture

Sustained growth via social media is just a piece of the larger puzzle called life. It's essential to keep it balanced with our offline existence. Maintain the equilibrium by ensuring that social media learning is complementary to your overall life goals; it should aid and not dominate your existence.

In conclusion, social media platforms lend themselves as powerful tools for lifelong learning and sustained growth. Keep the fire of curiosity alive, leverage the learning tools, manage plateaus and information overload, and keep your online growth balanced with your offline life. It's a marathon, not a sprint — take one day at a time, one step at a time, celebrating every milestone and victory. Keep growing, keep evolving.